EXPRESS YOURSELF!

Joyful Journaling for Kids

Christine Boucher

Design by Suzanne Good Hazard

Dover Publications, Inc.

Mineola, New York

To my husband, Dan, thank you for your unwavering love and support.

To my kids and greatest teachers, Jason, Ryan, & Sharon.

To Lisa, Suzanne, and Diane for helping me turn my dream into a reality.

And to Katey & Whiskers who sit by my side while I write.

Bibliographical Note

Express Yourself! Joyful Journaling for Kids is a new work, first published by Dover Publications, Inc., in 2020.

International Standard Book Number

ISBN-13: 978-0-486-83725-3
ISBN-10: 0-486-83725-4

Manufactured in the United States by LSC Communications
83725401
www.doverpublications.com

2 4 6 8 10 9 7 5 3 1
2019

To keep joy and happiness flowing . . .

This journal can be completed in any order. So flip through the pages and pick a section that speaks to you first. There are suggestions on how to fill out each chapter, but remember that this is *your* journal—do it your way and make it your own. Feel free to cross out topics that don't relate to you, and replace them with topics and ideas that are more on target with who you are. And if you don't understand something, ask an adult or a good friend to help you out. Don't forget to have fun decorating the pages with color, doodles, photos, or original art.

Before you dive in, here are some things to have on hand: pens, pencils, markers or crayons, stickers, photos, magazine pictures, ticket stubs, ribbons, awards, and other keepsakes that inspire you.

Chapter 1

JOYFUL ♥ JOTS

To keep joy & happiness flowing. . .

Write one word, draw one picture, or add something special to each box.

Think of something that makes you feel good about each topic listed on the following pages. If you come across any you don't like or know about, skip them or cross them out and add your own subject.

Example:

Vacation

Swimming

ONE WORD JOTS

66 "There are only two ways to live your life. One is as though nothing is a miracle. The other is as though everything is a miracle."

— Albert Einstein
Physicist

Write one or more positive words about each topic.

Winter	Spring
Summer	Fall

My Town

Playgrounds

Beaches

Parks

Write one or more positive words about each topic.

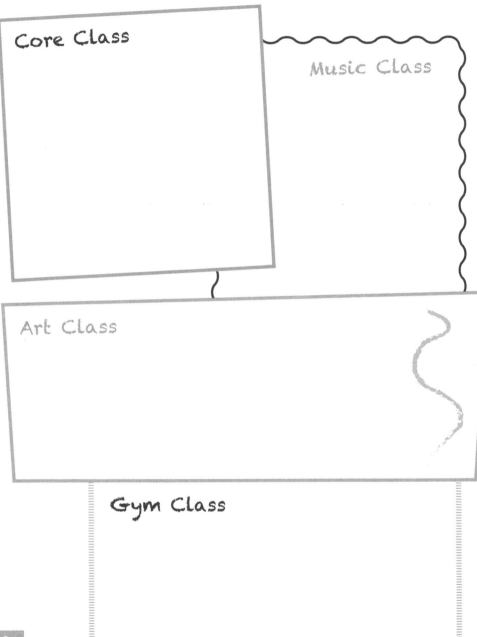

Core Class

Music Class

Art Class

Gym Class

Summer Vacations

Winter Vacations

Spring Vacations

Fall Vacations

Write one or more positive words about each topic.

School Days

My Teachers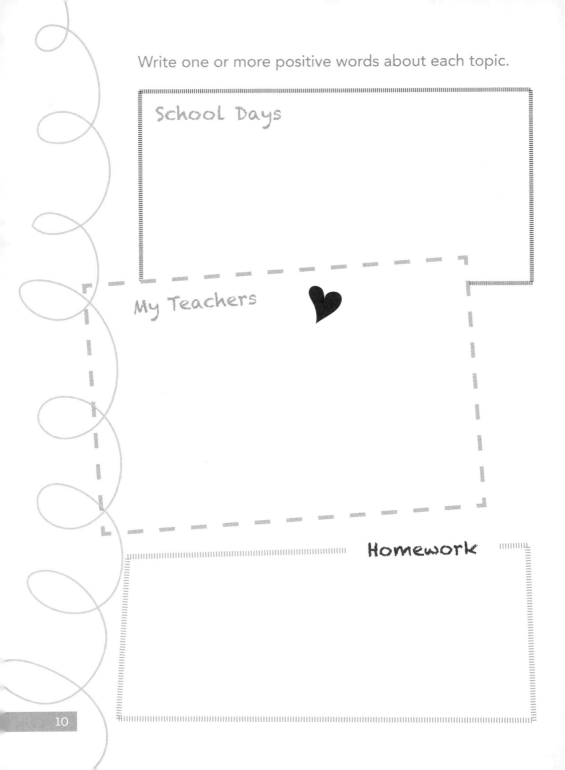

Homework

TV shows

Movies

Video Games

YouTube

Write one or more positive words about each topic.

Bedtime

Getting Up in the Morning

Staying Up Late

Sleeping In

Sunny Days

Snowy Days

Rainy Days

Windy Days

Write one or more positive words about each topic.

Your Hair

Your Eyes

Your Smile

Your Personality

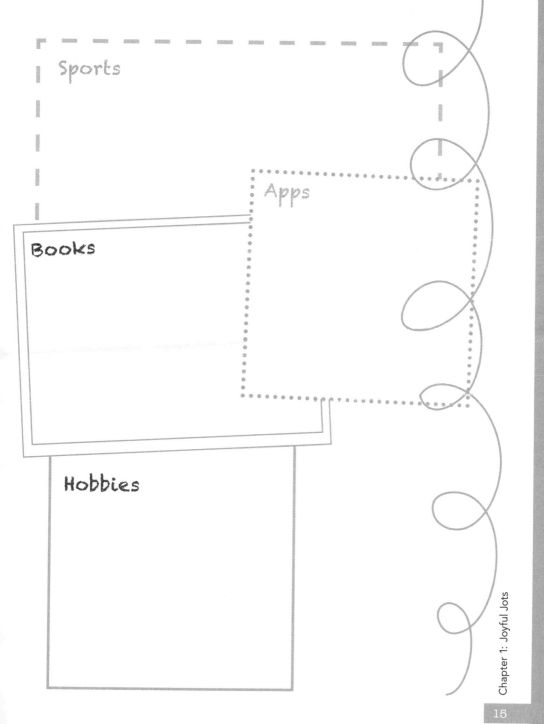

Sports

Apps

Books

Hobbies

Write one or more positive words about each topic.

Birthdays

Special Person's Birthday

_____
(name)

_____
(date)

Special Person's Birthday

_____
(name)

_____
(date)

Special Person's Birthday

_____
(name)

_____
(date)

My Room

Kitchen

Family Room

Special Hang-Out Place

Write one or more positive words about each topic.

Best Friend(s)

Good Friend(s)

School Friend(s)

New Friend(s)

Holiday: _____

Holiday: ....

Holiday: ~~~~~~~~~~~~~~~~~~

Write one or more positive words about each topic.

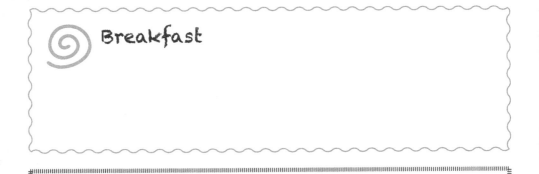

Breakfast

Lunch

Dinner

Holiday Meal

Write one or more positive words about each topic.

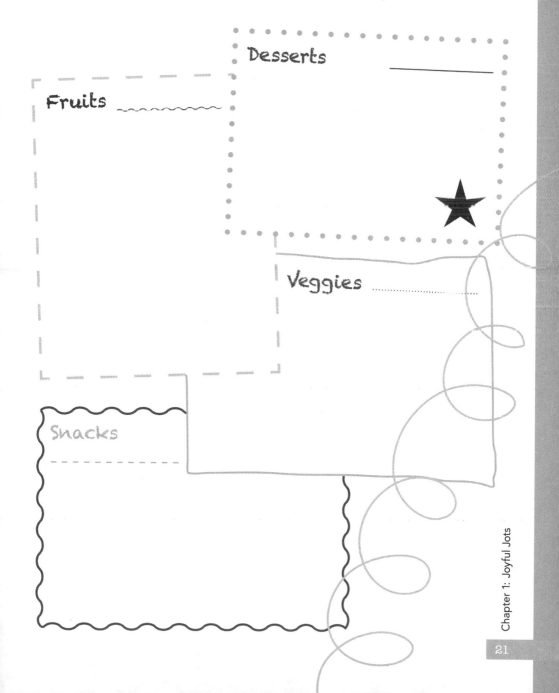

Desserts _____

Fruits ~~~~~~~~~

Veggies ....

Snacks

Chapter 2

@ MY FAVORITES

jot down 1 word, or a few words, describing your favorites!

Don't worry about what others think.
Dig deep and find your own likes.
Feel free to skip blocks and come back.

Example:

Animal

monkey

MY FAVORITES

" To be yourself in a world that is constantly trying to make you something else is the greatest accomplishment.**"**

— Ralph Waldo Emerson
Essayist

Add your favorites to the frames on pages 24–27.

Color

Animal

Food

Movie

TV show

Celebrity

App

Video
Game

Actor

Actress

Athlete

Musician

Book

Quiet
Spot

Winter
Fun

Summer
Fun

Fall
Fun

Spring
Fun

Indoor
Fun

Outdoor
Fun

Choose your own favorites!

FAVORITE THINGS I DO WITH:

Mom

Dad

Brother(s)

Sister(s)

"The bond that links your true family is not one of blood, but of respect and joy in each other's life."
— Richard Bach
Author

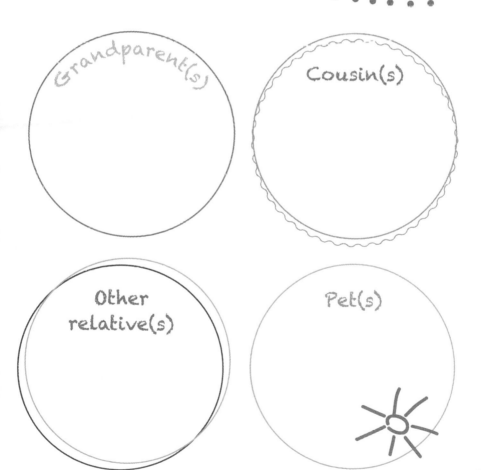

Grandparent(s)

Cousin(s)

Other relative(s)

Pet(s)

PICTURE IT!

Add pictures or make your own drawings
of your favorite things in the frames.

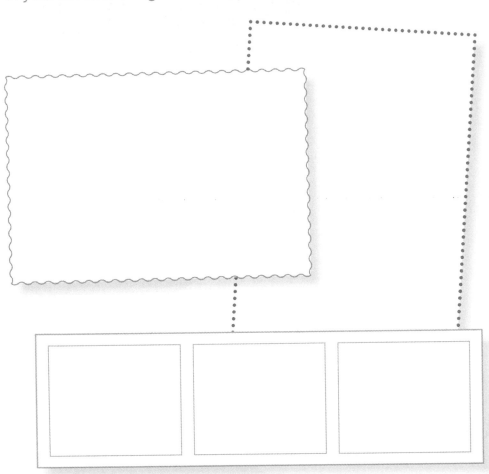

More Favorites:

Chapter

LOTS OF ?? QUESTIONS ???

Answer the questions in this chapter to get to know yourself better. You can add pictures or make your own drawings in the frames.

ALL ABOUT ME

Do you have a pet? Yes! No

If you don't have a pet, imagine one! Would you like one? What kind?

Name of my pet(s):

....

What do you like about your pet(s)?

1. ....

2. ....

3. ....

4. ....

5. ....

"An animal's eyes have the power to speak a great language."

– Martin Buber
Philosopher

Draw or add pictures of your pet(s).

My Good Friends

Names:

What makes these friends special?

"A friend is someone who knows all about you and still loves you."

– Elbert Hubbard
Writer

Draw or add pictures of your friends.

"Friendship with one's self is all-important, because without it one cannot be friends with anyone else in the world."

— Eleanor Roosevelt
First Lady

Sometimes we like to be with people, and sometimes we just want to be alone. What do you like to do alone? (Watch TV, read)

Favorite things to do with friends:

♥ _____

♥ _____

♥ _____

♥ _____

♥ _____

♥ _____

♥ _____

♥ _____

♥ _____

> **"Life isn't about finding yourself. Life is about creating yourself."**
>
> — George Bernard Shaw
> *Playwright*

Check one:

◯ I have my own room

◯ I share a room with: _____

What do you like about your room?

1. _____
2. _____
3. _____
4. _____

Is there anything that you would like to change about your room? (Examples: furniture, different paint colors, pictures). Write, draw or cut out pictures to show your ideas below.

What color walls will you choose?

FAMILY RELATIONSHIPS

How would you describe your parent(s)?

How would your parent(s) describe you?

PARENTS

My parents make
me feel...

_____

_____

_____

_____

_____

_____

I think I make
my parents feel...

_____

_____

_____

_____

_____

_____

_____

What can you do
to make your
relationship better?

_____

_____

_____

_____

_____

_____

What can your
parents do to make
your relationship
better?

_____

_____

_____

_____

_____

_____

66 Be who you are and say how you feel, because those who mind don't matter and those who matter don't mind."

— Bernard M. Baruch
Businessman

Other people probably think I am...

_____

_____

_____

_____

_____

_____

_____

Do you believe what they think?

◯ Yes!   ◯ No

Why, or why not?

~~~~~~

~~~~~~

~~~~~~

~~~~~~

~~~~~~

Does it really matter what people think?
Why, or why not?

....

....

....

....

....

....

OTHERS

" I do believe that if you haven't learnt about sadness, you cannot appreciate happiness."

— Nana Mouskouri
Singer

What are some things that make you sad?

....

....

....

Can you find peace with these sad feelings?

◯ Yes!   ◯ No

"It's okay to be sad. Everyone gets sad now and then. Even me."

– Nicholas Sparks
Novelist

Can you change the things that make you sad? How?

~~~~~~

~~~~~~

~~~~~~

> **"The only mistake you can make is not asking for help."**
> — Sandeep Jauhar
> *Author*

If you can't change the things that make you sad, is there someone you can go to for help?

 Yes   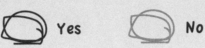 No

Who would you go to for help?

....

I trust this person because...

~~~~~~

~~~~~~

~~~~~~

> **[Friendship is born at the moment that one person says to another]: "What! You too? I thought I was the only one."**
> — C.S. Lewis, *The Four Loves*
> *Author*

secret noun
se·cret | \sē-krət\

Something kept from the knowledge of others or shared confidentially with a few.

— *Merriam-Webster Dictionary*

Have you ever trusted someone with a secret that they told other people? ◯ Yes ◯ No

If yes, it made me feel...

❝ Love all, trust a few, do wrong to none."

— William Shakespeare
Playwright and Poet

Looking back:

 I should have kept my secret to myself.

 I should have trusted someone else.

 I won't share my secrets with this person again.

 I'll be more careful who I share my secrets with.

What positive things have you learned from sharing your secret?

~~~~~~

~~~~~~

~~~~~~

Have you ever told someone else's secret?

◯ Yes   ◯ No

Why?

....

....

....

....

> "A true friend will keep your secrets and love you without judgment or conditions."
>
> – Unknown

How did it make you feel?

Sometimes we have to tell someone's secret in order to help that person. Has this ever happened to you?

 Yes   No

Write about that time:

. . . .

. . . .

. . . .

. . . .

> "We can't help everyone, but everyone can help someone."
>
> — Ronald Reagan
> *U.S. President*

Do you wish someone had told one of your secrets to help you?

 Yes   No

How might it have helped you?

. . . .

. . . .

. . . .

. . . .

EXPERIENCES

Think of a negative experience you've had. Did you learn something from it? Did you learn something that you should NOT do?

Example:

Experience: _I got my screen time taken away for a week because I lied to my parents._

What I learned: _My parents were mad at me more for lying than for sneaking extra screen time. If I hadn't lied, maybe they would have been more understanding._

Experience: ....

....

What I learned: ....

....

....

....

> "Always turn a negative situation into a positive situation."
>
> – Michael Jordan
> *Basketball player*

Experience: ....

....

What I learned: ....

....

....

....

Experience:

What I learned:

MISTAKES HAPPEN

Sometimes we make mistakes. All mistakes are learning experiences. Take some time to think about mistakes that you have made.

Describe a mistake you made:

Did you know you were making a mistake beforehand? If yes, why did you continue to do it? If not, when did you realize it was a mistake?

> "Anyone who has never made a mistake has never tried anything new."
> — Albert Einstein
> *Physicist*

How did you feel after making the mistake?

( ) Sad

( ) Silly

( ) Disappointed

( ) Embarrassed

( ) Okay

( ) _____

What were the consequences of your mistake?

- -

- -

- -

- -

- -

> **"** The only real mistake is the one from which we learn nothing."
>
> — Henry Ford
> *Automotive Pioneer*

Everyone makes mistakes. Everyone messes up sometimes. The key is to learn from your mistakes.

Think about some of the mistakes you've made — then take some time to fill in the next few pages.

Example:

I made a mistake by *yelling at my brother.*

I learned that *I really hurt his feelings.*

Next time I will *try to take some deep breaths to calm myself down before talking to him about going into my room.*

I made a mistake by _____

I learned that _____

Next time I will _____

_____

_____

~~~~~~

I made a mistake by _____

I learned that _____

Next time I will _____

_____

_____

~~~~~~

I made a mistake by _____

I learned that _____

Next time I will _____

_____

_____

OH SO EMBARRASSING!

We've all had those moments when we just want to hide and hope that no one saw or heard us do that embarrassing thing!

Fill in the circles with some of your most embarrassing moments.

I was embarrassed because...

_____

_____

It made me feel... _____

_____

_____

I was embarrassed because...

_____

_____

It made me feel... _____

_____

_____

I was embarrassed because...

_____

_____

It made me feel... _____

_____

_____

I was embarrassed because...

_____

_____

It made me feel... _____

_____

_____

I was embarrassed because...

_____

_____

It made me feel... _____

_____

_____

Chapter 4

DREAM
BIG!

These next few pages encourage you to...

Dream big and believe in the possibilities that life has to offer!

Do you dream of buying yourself a new phone or bike? Or do you think about exploring the Grand Canyon, zip lining above a tropical rain forest, going into outer space, or fighting crime when you get older? Or perhaps your goal is to become a successful author or athlete, or a famous scientist, politician, actor, or rock star. Whether you dream of something you want to have or want to do, it helps to write about it. So take some time to think about future goals and how you might achieve them. Then fill in the blanks and set these dreams in motion!

" It takes courage to grow up and become who you really are."

— E.E. Cummings
Poet

I dream of being _____
when I'm older.

What steps can you take to achieve
this dream?

~~~~~~~~~~~~~~~~~~~~~~~~

~~~~~~~~~~~~~~~~~~~~~~~~

~~~~~~~~~~~~~~~~~~~~~~~~

"If you do what you love,
you'll never work a day
in your life."

— Anonymous

~~~~~~

~~~~~~

"The future belongs to those who believe in the beauty of their dreams."

– Eleanor Roosevelt
First Lady

Draw or add pictures that inspire you to achieve this goal!

It's common for people to have more than one dream, or for goals to change over time. What you want today might not be the same thing you dream about next year. With this in mind, here are some pages for you to list additional ambitions for yourself. The key is to be aware of your thoughts, be excited about your goals, and do not get discouraged if you encounter difficulties along the way to achieving them.

66 Never underestimate the power of dreams and the influence of the human spirit. We are all the same in this notion: The potential for greatness lives within each of us."

– Wilma Rudolph
Olympic Champion

Fill in what your dream is:

Something I dream of doing or having is...................................

.... because..

....

To have my dream come true would be.....................................

....

....

Fill in what your dream is:

Something I dream of doing or having is...................................

.... because..

....

To have my dream come true would be ....

....

....

MY GOAL GARDENS

" It's impossible," said pride.

"It's risky," said experience.

"It's pointless," said reason.

"Give it a try," whispered the heart.

— Anonymous

On the next few pages are Goal Gardens—places to help you visualize your dreams. Starting at the top, write in the main idea of the goal you would like to achieve. Next, fill in steps 1–4 with ways to help you reach your goal—Goal Garden #1 is an example of how to fill it out. Then get started working toward your goal!

GOAL GARDEN #1

Main Idea: ......To get better grades..................................

I reached my
GOAL!!!

Step #4:

Come prepared
to all my
classes.

Step #3:

Ask for help
if I need it.

Step #2:

Study every
weeknight.

Step #1:

Cut down on my screen time.

START HERE

GOAL GARDEN #2

Main Idea: ....

I reached my
GOAL!!!

Step #4:

. . . .

. . . .

. . . .

Step #3:

. . . .

. . . .

. . . .

Step #2:

. . . .

. . . .

. . . .

Step #1:

. . . .

START HERE

GOAL GARDEN #3

Main Idea: ....

I reached my
GOAL!!!

Step #4:

. . . .

. . . .

. . . .

Step #3:

. . . .

. . . .

. . . .

Step #2:

. . . .

. . . .

. . . .

Step #1:

. . . .

START HERE

Chapter 5

POSITIVE ♥ VIBES

Now focus on how to talk to yourself and others in a positive way.
Let joy and positivity lift your spirits!

"A positive attitude causes a chain reaction of positive thoughts, events and outcomes. It is a catalyst and it sparks extraordinary results."

— Wade Boggs
Baseball player

POSITIVE "I AM'S"

"I am" statements are very powerful. Whatever you think and say can influence what you become and how you feel. Spend some time filling in the blanks with positive statements about yourself. Once you have filled out a few lines, repeat these statements to yourself throughout your day. Do this exercise often.

Examples:

→ I am smart.

→ I am lovable.

→ I am honest.

→ I am deserving.

→ I am a loyal friend.

→ I am a loving son/daughter.

→ I am responsible.

→ I am a good sport.

→ I am excellent at math.

→ I am a fine musician.

→ I am a talented artist.

→ I am a hard-working student.

→ I am kind.

→ I am brave.

→ I am polite.

→ I am patient.

→ I am a good athlete.

I AM

I AM

I AM

I AM

I AM

I AM

I AM

I AM

I AM

I AM

I AM

I AM

I AM

I AM

List all of the things you are good at.

I am good at

I am good at

I am good at

I am good at

I am good at

I am good at

I am good at

I am good at

I am good at

I am good at

I am good at

I am good at

Fill in the blanks with some of the things you are working on getting better at.

Example:

I AM GETTING BETTER AT *keeping my room clean* .

I AM GETTING BETTER AT

I AM GETTING BETTER AT

I AM GETTING BETTER AT

I AM GETTING BETTER AT

I AM GETTING BETTER AT

I AM GETTING BETTER AT

"**Once you replace negative thoughts with positive ones, you'll start having positive results.**"

– Willie Nelson
Musician

Can you switch your negative thoughts into positive ones?

Spend time each day recognizing when your thoughts turn negative. Take time to switch those thoughts into positive ones.

Examples:

I _stink at math._

(negative thought)

Switch that thought to:

I _know I'll get better if I work at it._

(positive thought)

I _am a horrible artist._

(negative thought)

Switch that thought to:

I _am creative in different ways._

(positive thought)

I _don't have a lot of friends._

(negative thought)

Switch that thought to:

The friends I have are super-special.

(positive thought)

SWITCH-IT!

Here are some pages to work on switching your negative thoughts.

I _____ (negative thought)

Switch that thought to:

I _____ (positive thought)

I _____ (negative thought)

Switch that thought to:

I _____ (positive thought)

I _____ (negative thought)

Switch that thought to:

I _____ (positive thought)

I _____
(negative thought)

Switch that thought to:

I _____
(positive thought)

I _____
(negative thought)

Switch that thought to:

I _____
(positive thought)

I _____
(negative thought)

Switch that thought to:

I _____
(positive thought)

I _____
(negative thought)

Switch that thought to:

I _____
(positive thought)

I _____
(negative thought)

Switch that thought to:

I _____
(positive thought)

Chapter 5: Positive Vibes

"Every time you put something positive into the universe, the world changes. Your kindness invites miracles to show up, not just in your world, but in the whole world."

— unknown

Whatever you do or say comes back to you in some way. It may not come back exactly the same, but if you spread negativity, you will most likely get negativity back. But if you spread kindness and happiness, you usually will get kindness and happiness in return.

POSITIVE ☺ ☹ NEGATIVE

Caring

Happiness

Kindness

Joy

Love

Forgiveness

Trust

Hate

Anger

Cruelty

Greed

Selfishness

Jealousy

Think about positive and negative words (examples on page 81). Which words describe what you want to send out into the world?

"If positivity is what you put out in the universe, positivity is what you get."

– Demi Lovato
Singer

Example:

I want to put _caring_ into the world.

I want to put _____ into the world.

I want to put _____ into the world.

I want to put _____ into the world.

What types of people do you want in your life? Friendly? Kind? Trustworthy?

> **" If you put the right things into the universe, the right things will come to you."**
>
> **– Jena Malone**
> *Actress*

What things do you want to come back to you?
Fill in the blanks on the next few pages.

Examples:

I want __friendly people in my life__ ,

so I am __friendly__ _____ to others.

I want __Kind people in my life__ ,

so I am __Kind__ _____ to others.

I want ....,

so I am .... to others.

I want ....,

so I am .... to others.

I want ....,

so I am .... to others.

I want ....,

so I am .... to others.

I want ————————————————— ,

so I am ————————————— to others.

I want ——————————————————— ,

so I am ———— ———————————— to others.

I want ————————————————— ,

so I am ——————————————— to others.

I want ——————————————————— ,

so I am ————————————————— to others.

MINDFUL MEDITATION

Thinking positive thoughts about yourself, the people you love as well as the people you "don't like so much," and the world around you can help you to feel good and let go of the grudges and anger that we sometimes hold inside.

The following meditation exercise can help people relax and de-stress. Try it while sitting quietly by yourself. You might want to do this exercise before you go to bed and drift off to sleep. Hopefully, it will become part of a daily routine to do whenever, and wherever, you can.

STEP #1: While focusing on yourself, repeat the following:

May I be safe.
May I be happy.
May I be healthy.
May I be at peace.

These are all things that you deserve and are worthy of having.

STEP #2: Fill in the blanks with the name of someone you love — then repeat the following:

May _____ be safe.
May _____ be happy.
May _____ be healthy.
May _____ be at peace.

These are all things that they deserve and are worthy of having.

STEP #3: Fill in the blanks with the name of someone you don't "like" very much — then repeat the following:

May _____ be safe.
May _____ be happy.
May _____ be healthy.
May _____ be at peace.

Focusing positive thoughts on the people who hurt your feelings can help release your negative feelings about them.

STEP #4: Envision your neighborhood, community, or even the whole world — sit quietly and say:

May we be safe.
May we be happy.
May we be healthy.
May we be at peace.

Keep the good vibe going by sitting quietly for a few moments afterward.

Feeling good or need more practice? On the following pages you'll find some extras to fill in.

STEP #1: While focusing on yourself, repeat the following:

May I be safe.
May I be happy.
May I be healthy.
May I be at peace.

These are all things that you deserve and are worthy of having.

STEP #2: Fill in the blanks with the name of someone you love — then repeat the following:

May _____ be safe.
May _____ be happy.
May _____ be healthy.
May _____ be at peace.

These are all things that they deserve and are worthy of having.

STEP #3: Fill in the blanks with the name of someone you don't "like" very much — then repeat the following:

May _____ be safe.
May _____ be happy.
May _____ be healthy.
May _____ be at peace.

Focusing positive thoughts on the people who hurt your feelings can help release your negative feelings about them.

STEP #4: Envision your neighborhood, community, or even the whole world — sit quietly and say:

May we be safe.
May we be happy.
May we be healthy.
May we be at peace.

Keep the good vibe going by sitting quietly for a few moments afterward.

STEP #1: While focusing on yourself, repeat the following:

May I be safe.
May I be happy.
May I be healthy.
May I be at peace.

These are all things that you deserve and are worthy of having.

STEP #2: Fill in the blanks with the name of someone you love — then repeat the following:

May _____ be safe.
May _____ be happy.
May _____ be healthy.
May _____ be at peace.

These are all things that they deserve and are worthy of having.

STEP #3: Fill in the blanks with the name of someone you don't "like" very much — then repeat the following:

May _____ be safe.
May _____ be happy.
May _____ be healthy.
May _____ be at peace.

Focusing positive thoughts on the people who hurt your feelings can help release your negative feelings about them.

STEP #4: Envision your neighborhood, community, or even the whole world — sit quietly and say:

May we be safe.
May we be happy.
May we be healthy.
May we be at peace.

Keep the good vibe going by sitting quietly for a few moments afterward.

Chapter

FEELING ♥

GOOD!!

The prompts on the following pages will help you focus on different types of feelings. Some days you might feel happy, grateful, sad, unsure of yourself, or angry.

" The best and most beautiful things in the world cannot be seen or even touched. They must be felt with the heart."

— Helen Keller
Author

WHAT MAKES YOU HAPPY?

Take time to write down things that make you feel happy. You don't have to fill out all of these lines right now—come back to these pages whenever you want.

Example:

When I *hang out with Sharon* I feel happy.

> **"** Folks are usually about as happy as they make their minds up to be. **"**
>
> — Abraham Lincoln
> U.S. President

When I .... I feel happy.

When I .... I feel happy.

When I .... I feel happy.

When I .... I feel happy.

When I .... I feel happy.

When I .... I feel happy.

When I .... I feel happy.

When I .... I feel happy.

When I .... I feel happy.

When I .... I feel happy.

When I .... I feel happy.

When I .... I feel happy.

When I .... I feel happy.

When I .... I feel happy.

When I .... I feel happy.

WHAT AM I GRATEFUL FOR?

" Feeling gratitude and not expressing it is like wrapping a present and not giving it."

— William Arthur Ward
Writer

Fill in the blanks below listing what you feel grateful for—it can be a person, place, or thing. You can do this today, next week, or even next month. Take your time and enjoy the good feeling of being grateful.

Examples:

I am grateful for *my family* .

I am grateful for *my best friends, Will & Ben* .

I am grateful for *my new ballet shoes* .

I am grateful for *pizza* .

I am grateful for *sunshine* .

I am grateful for

I am grateful for

I am grateful for

I am grateful for

I am grateful for

I am grateful for

I am grateful for

I am grateful for

I am grateful for

I am grateful for

I am grateful for

I am grateful for

WHAT DO YOU LOVE?

Fill in the blanks with the things you love.

Examples:

I love *it when my mom or dad hugs me*.

I love *my big brother, Jason*.

I love _____.

I love _____.

I love _____.

I love _____.

I love _____.

I love _____.

I love _____.

I love _____.

I love _____.

I love _____.

I love _____.

"**If you judge people, you have no time to love them.**"

— **Mother Teresa**
Nun and Missionary

PICTURE IT!

Draw or add pictures of people, places, and things that you love.

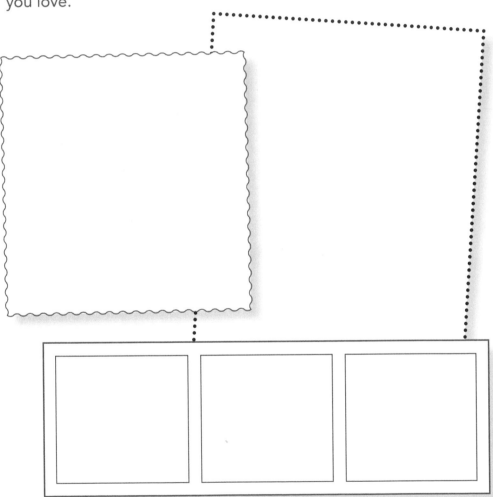

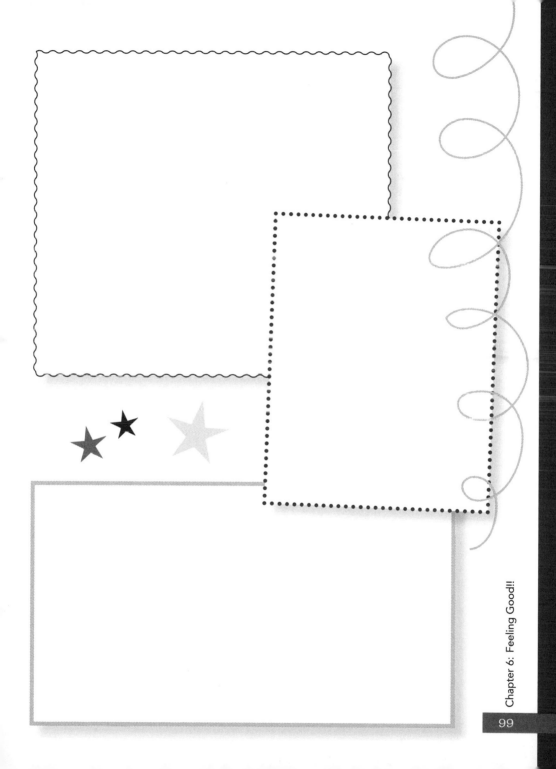

WHAT DO YOU ENJOY?

"When you enjoy what you do, work becomes play." – Martin Yan
Chef and Author

Take the time to focus on the things that you enjoy.

Examples:

I enjoy *reading mysteries* .

I enjoy *playing soccer* .

I enjoy _____ .

I enjoy _____ .

I enjoy _____ .

I enjoy _____ .

I enjoy _____ .

I enjoy _____ .

I enjoy _____ .

I enjoy _____ .

HOW CAN YOU SPREAD HAPPINESS?

> "I've learned that people will forget what you said, people will forget what you did, but people will never forget how you made them feel."
> — Maya Angelou
> Poet

I can spread happiness by _calling my grandma_ .

I can spread happiness by _____ .

I can spread happiness by _____ .

I can spread happiness by _____ .

I can spread happiness by _____ .

I can spread happiness by _____ .

I can spread happiness by _____ .

I can spread happiness by _____ .

I can spread happiness by _____ .

I can spread happiness by _____ .

TRUST YOUR INSTINCTS

In order to trust your instincts, you have to get in touch with how you feel. Feelings can help you to make good decisions. Fill in the blanks to practice getting in touch with your feelings.

Examples:

Right now, I feel *sad* **because**

Coach hurt my feelings .

This tells me *I need to talk to her about how I want to be treated* .

Right now, I feel *happy* **because**

my mom surprised me with a trip to the movies .

This tells me *that my mom wants to spend time with me* .

Right now, I feel _____ **because**

_____ .

This tells me _____ .

Right now, I feel ....

because ....

....

This tells me ....

....

Right now, I feel .... because

....

This tells me ....

Right now, I feel .... because

....

This tells me ....

Right now, I feel .... because

....

This tells me ....

HELPING OTHERS

Helping others benefits both the giver and the receiver. Fill in the blanks as a reminder of how it feels to help someone.

Example:

I helped _Ryan_ today by _picking up his books_
when he dropped them .
It made me feel _good about myself_ .

I helped _____ today by _____
_____ .
It made me feel _____ .

I helped _____ today by _____
_____ .
It made me feel _____ .

I helped ~~~~~~~~~~ today by ~~~~~~~~~~~

~~~~~~~~~~~~~~~~~~~~~~~~~~~~~~~~~~ .

It made me feel ~~~~~~~~~~~~~~~~~~~~~~~ .

I helped ~~~~~~~~~~ today by ~~~~~~~~~~~

~~~~~~~~~~~~~~~~~~~~~~~~~~~~~~~~~~ .

It made me feel ~~~~~~~~~~~~~~~~~~~~~~~ .

I helped ~~~~~~~~~~ today by ~~~~~~~~~~~

~~~~~~~~~~~~~~~~~~~~~~~~~~~~~~~~~~ .

It made me feel ~~~~~~~~~~~~~~~~~~~~~~~ .

I helped ~~~~~~~~~~ today by ~~~~~~~~~~~

~~~~~~~~~~~~~~~~~~~~~~~~~~~~~~~~~~ .

It made me feel ~~~~~~~~~~~~~~~~~~~~~~~ .

I helped ~~~~~~~~~~ today by ~~~~~~~~~~~

~~~~~~~~~~~~~~~~~~~~~~~~~~~~~~~~~~ .

It made me feel ~~~~~~~~~~~~~~~~~~~~~~~ .

MOVING ON!

" Every day is a new day, and you'll never be able to find happiness if you don't move on."

— Carrie Underwood
Singer

Sometimes moving on means accepting things that we can't change. Sometimes people can be mean, sometimes rules seem unfair, and sometimes things just don't go your way. Moving on from an unhappy situation can help you feel better!

Example:

I'm moving on from *Leah and her hurtful comments about me*

because *it will make me feel better*

.

I'm moving on from ‿‿‿‿‿‿‿‿‿‿‿‿‿‿‿‿‿

because ‿‿‿‿‿‿‿‿‿‿‿‿‿‿‿‿‿‿‿‿‿

‿‿‿‿‿‿‿‿‿‿‿‿‿‿‿‿‿‿‿‿‿‿‿ .

I'm moving on from ‿‿‿‿‿‿‿‿‿‿‿‿‿‿‿‿‿

because ‿‿‿‿‿‿‿‿‿‿‿‿‿‿‿‿‿‿‿‿‿

‿‿‿‿‿‿‿‿‿‿‿‿‿‿‿‿‿‿‿‿‿‿‿ .

I'm moving on from ‿‿‿‿‿‿‿‿‿‿‿‿‿‿‿‿‿

because ‿‿‿‿‿‿‿‿‿‿‿‿‿‿‿‿‿‿‿‿‿

‿‿‿‿‿‿‿‿‿‿‿‿‿‿‿‿‿‿‿‿‿‿‿ .

I'm moving on from ‿‿‿‿‿‿‿‿‿‿‿‿‿‿‿‿‿

because ‿‿‿‿‿‿‿‿‿‿‿‿‿‿‿‿‿‿‿‿‿

‿‿‿‿‿‿‿‿‿‿‿‿‿‿‿‿‿‿‿‿‿‿‿ .

I'm moving on from ‿‿‿‿‿‿‿‿‿‿‿‿‿‿‿‿‿

because ‿‿‿‿‿‿‿‿‿‿‿‿‿‿‿‿‿‿‿‿‿

‿‿‿‿‿‿‿‿‿‿‿‿‿‿‿‿‿‿‿‿‿‿‿ .

FORGIVENESS

Forgiveness can be hard, but try to do it for yourself. Forgiveness doesn't mean that you should continue to let someone hurt you, but that you are letting go of the negative feelings you are holding on to. This can bring you peace and allow more opportunities for happiness in your life.

Examples:

I forgive _Mark_ for _not inviting to me to_ _his party_ because _I don't like feeling_ _angry anymore_ .

I forgive _Kate_ for _hurting my feelings_ because _she said she's sorry and_ _I still want to be friends with her_ .

I forgive _____ for _____ because _____ .

"Forgiveness is a gift you give yourself."

– Tony Robbins
Author

I forgive _____

for _____

because _____

_____ .

I forgive _____

for _____

because _____

_____ .

I forgive _____ for _____

_____ because _____

_____ .

I forgive _____ for _____

_____ because _____

_____ .

I forgive _____ for _____

_____ because _____

_____ .

Awesome Activities!

These fun activities will help lift your spirits and show you how positivity can become part of your everyday life!

These projects will require a bit more time and some materials, so you might want to gather together magazines, photographs, poster board, markers, glue, and other craft supplies, along with your joyful thoughts and enthusiasm.

WHO ARE YOU?

" Today you are You, that is truer than true. There is no one else alive who is Youer than You."

— Dr. Seuss
Author

Draw or add a picture of yourself on this page.

Are you:

○ a math whiz? ○ an athlete?

○ a good friend? ○ a hard worker?

○ a musician? ○ all of these?

○ I am a(n) ~~~~~~~~~~~~~~~~~~~~~~~~~.

Use this space to showcase your personality with pictures and words.

SURROUNDED BY SUPPORT

"If you surround yourself with positive people who build you up, the sky is the limit."

– Joel Brown
Entrepreneur

It feels good to know that you are surrounded by people who are positive and to whom you can turn for support. Fill in the blanks with the names of people who are always there for you.

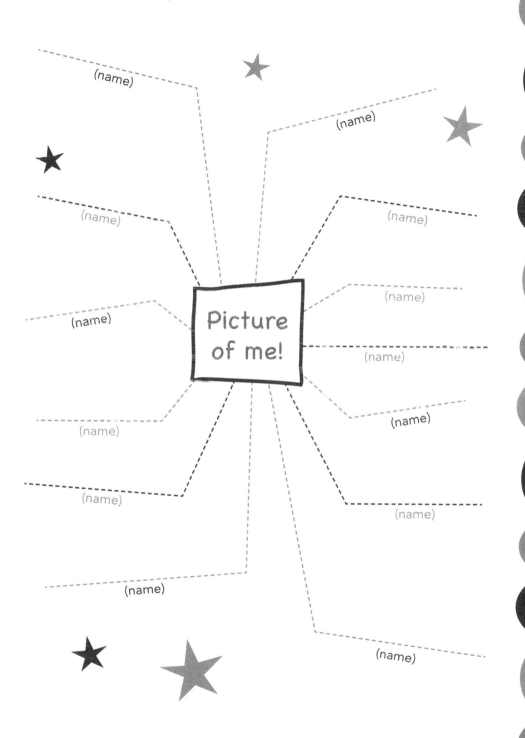

(name)

(name)

(name)

(name)

(name)

(name)

(name)

Picture of me!

(name)

(name)

(name)

(name)

(name)

DREAM BOARD

"We grow great by dreams."

— Woodrow Wilson
U.S. President

Create a poster-board collage showing all of the people, places, things, words, and feelings that you want to have in your life. Do you dream of being an actress, athlete, engineer, or police officer? Do you dream of going to college? Do you dream of having that amazing pair of shoes? Do you dream of taking an exciting vacation? This blank poster-board collage is your space to dream.

Gather your craft materials and get going!

Look at your board often and watch as your dreams start to come true.

QUOTE NOTES

> "All your dreams can come true if you have the courage to pursue them."
> — Walt Disney
> *Animated film pioneer and theme park founder*

Cut out a positive quote note that speaks to you. Carry it with you and read it several times throughout your day. Notice how you feel when you read these positive statements.

Why not pass along a note to a friend or family member who could use a pick-me-up? Hide it in a lunch bag, coat pocket, or enclose it in a card. You can even snap a photo of a favorite quote and message it to them.

The quotes on the next couple of pages come from writers, sports figures, political activists, and others who have shared their wisdom with the world.

"It's not what
happens to you, but
how you react
to it that matters."

— Epictetus

"Winning doesn't
always mean being first.
Winning means you're
doing better than you've
done before."

— Bonnie Blair

"You must be
the change you
wish to see in
the world."

— Mahatma Gandhi

"I am only one, but I am one.
I cannot do everything, but I can
do something. And I will not
let what I cannot do interfere with
what I can do."

— Edward Everett Hale

"It always seems
Impossible until
it's done."

— Nelson Mandela

"To accomplish great
things, we must not only
act, but also dream,
not only plan, but
also believe."

— Anatole France

"Don't let what
you cannot do
interfere with
what you can do."

— John Wooden

"No one is
perfect – that's
why pencils
have erasers."

— Wolfgang Riebe

"If they don't like you
for being yourself,
be yourself even more."

— Taylor Swift

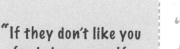

"IT'S OUR EMOTIONS
AND IMPERFECTIONS
THAT MAKE US
HUMAN."

— Clyde DeSouza

"You're braver than you
believe, stronger than
you seem, and smarter
than you think."

— A.A. Milne (Christopher Robin)

"You have been my friend . . . That in itself is a tremendous thing."

— E.B. White

"Keep your face always toward the sunshine—and shadows will fall behind you."

— Walt Whitman

"Try to be a rainbow in someone's cloud."

— Maya Angelou

"Positive thinking will let you do everything better than negative thinking will."

— Zig Ziglar

"Happiness is not out there for us to find. The reason that it's not out there is that it's inside us."

— Sonja Lyubomirsky

"YOU ARE ENOUGH JUST AS YOU ARE."

— Meghan Markle

"Don't worry about failures, worry about the chances you miss when you don't even try."

— Jack Canfield

"The weak can never forgive. Forgiveness is the attribute of the strong."

— Mahatma Gandhi

"Let us make our future now, and let us make our dreams tomorrow's reality."

— Malala Yousafzai

"If you have good thoughts they will shine out of your face like sunbeams and you will always look lovely."

— Roald Dahl

"There are no limits on what you can achieve with your life, except the limits you accept in your mind."

— Brian Tracy

"Don't be pushed around by the fears in your mind. Be led by the dreams in your heart."

— Roy T. Bennett

"Everything you can imagine is real."

— Pablo Picasso
Artist

"Learn from yesterday, live for today, hope for tomorrow."

— Albert Einstein
Physicist

"Why fit in when you were born to stand out?"

— Dr. Seuss
Author

CREATE A GRATITUDE JAR

"**Gratitude helps you to grow and expand; gratitude brings joy and laughter into your life and into the lives of all those around you.**" — Eileen Caddy
Author

Creating a gratitude jar is a fun project that serves as a reminder of all of the things that you are thankful for. Find a clean, empty jar and decorate it anyway you choose. It could be as simple as using a marker to write your name, or a more elaborate design using stickers, yarn, glitter, ribbon, photos, and other crafty items that will make it your own.

Cut out blank strips of paper and write, "I am grateful for
_____" on them. Fill out a gratitude strip once a
day, once a week, or whenever you think of something
that makes you happy, and put your paper in the jar. The
more pieces of paper you can complete, the faster your
jar will fill up.

At the end of a week, a month, or whenever you might
be feeling down, read all of your gratitude statements.
Reflecting on these happy moments can serve as a
reminder of how lucky you are and can help to lift
your spirits.

Examples:

I am grateful for _the support I get from my parents_.

I am grateful for _the weekend_____.

I am grateful for _my best friend_____.

I am grateful for _ice cream_____.

CREATE A WISHING BOX

"The most fantastic magical things can happen, and it all starts with a wish."

—Jiminy Cricket
(Pinocchio movie)

It's fun to dream and wish for all of the things that you would like to have or be. A wishing box is a great place to keep your wishes! To make your wishing box, find a small box with a lid and write on it "My Wishing Box." Be creative and decorate the box any way you want. Cut out some strips of paper or shapes (squares, stars, or circles would be fun!) and any time you wish for something, write: "I wish _____" and put it in the box.

Take a moment to imagine what it would be like if your wishes came true. Every now and then, go through the box and review your wishes. Did any come true? Never stop dreaming, and keep adding wishes!

Examples:

I wish _I could go on a summer vacation_ .

I wish

I could adopt

a dog .

I wish

I could learn to

play the piano .

Look for something positive in each day, even if some days you have to look a little harder . . .

You've come to the end of this journal, but it's really only the beginning. Keep these tools with you forever, because focusing on positivity and joy is an amazing way to live your life!